Backyard Books

Are you a Ladybug?

KINGFISHER

Larousse Kingfisher Chambers Inc.

95 Madison Avenue

New York, New York 10016

First published in 2000

3 5 7 9 10 8 6 4 2

2TR/0600/TWP/DIG/150NYMA

LIBRARY OF CONGRESS CATALOGING-IN-PUBLICATION DATA

Allen, Judy.

Are you a ladybug?/by Judy Allen; illustrated by Tudor Humphries.—1st ed.

p. cm. (Backyard Books)

Summary: Introduces the life cycle of a ladybug, showing how it changes from an egg
to an adult ladybug.

ISBN 0-7534-5241-3 (hb)

1. Ladybugs—Juvenile literature. [1. Ladybugs.] I. Title. II. Series. III. Humphries,
Tudor, ill.

QL596.C65 A46 2000

595.76'9 21—dc21

99-042381

Editor: Katie Puckett
Coordinating Editor: Laura Marshall
Series Designer: Jane Tassie

Printed in Singapore

Are You a Ladybug?

Judy Allen and Tudor Humphries

KING*f*ISHER

NEW YORK

Are you a ladybug?

If you are,
your parents look like this,
and they eat aphids.

When your
mother lays
her eggs, you are
inside one of them.

While you're
in there, you will
gr**OW**.

When you have grown big enough,
break out of the egg.

You have a lot of brothers and sisters.
If you look at them you might think
you have all made a big mistake.

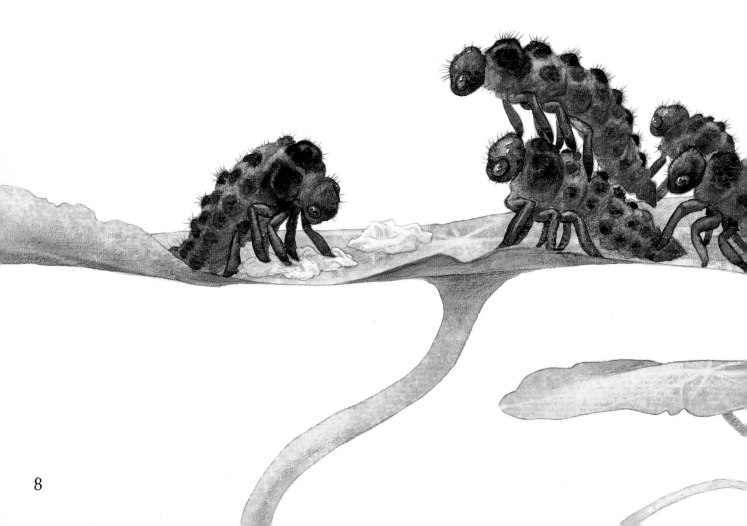

Not one of you is the same shape as a ladybug. Not one of you is the same color as a ladybug.

Don't worry about this. Just eat.

Eat your own eggshell first.

Then eat aphids.

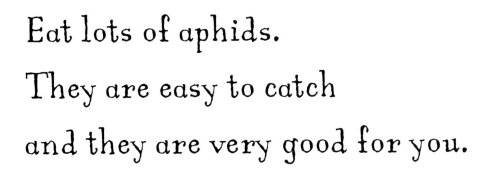

Eat lots of aphids.
They are easy to catch
and they are very good for you.

As you grow bigger,
your skin will feel tight.

This is not a problem.

Soon, it will split down the middle.

Wriggle out of it

and take it off.

Then eat more aphids.

As you grow, you must take off your skin again—and again. Each time there is a new one underneath.

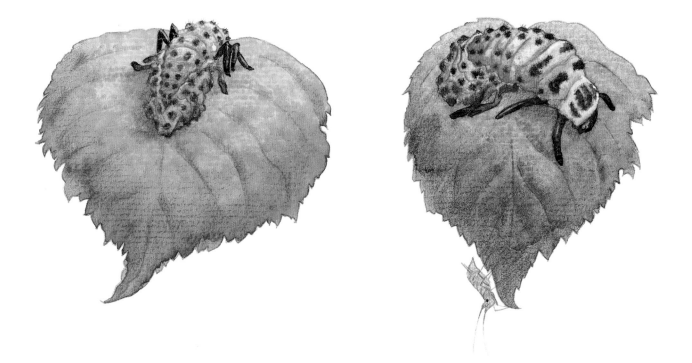

Keep eating the aphids.

One day you will feel very tired.
Stop eating. Curl up like this.

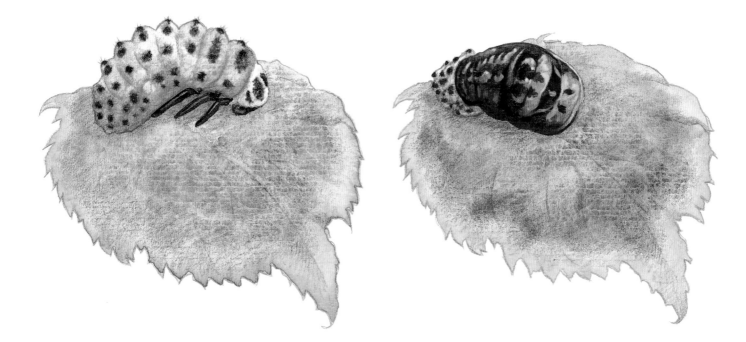

Take off your skin one more time.
Now wait for your new skin to grow hard.

When your hard skin splits,
climb out of it one last time.

Now you are the right shape,
but you are not the right color.
You are very, very pale.

Just wait...

Slowly,
slowly,
slowly,
your color
grows stronger.

Your black dots appear.

Congratulations,
you're a
ladybug!

You can fly!

You are very hungry,
so look for something to eat.

Aphids will do nicely.

23

However,
if your parents
look a little
like this

or this

or this

you are not a ladybug.

You are...

... a human child.

Your skin will not split as you grow.

You can't fly.

It is very unlikely that you
are red with black dots.

But you can do a lot of
things that ladybugs can't do.

And you will never, ever,
EVER have to eat aphids.

Did You Know...

...a female ladybug
can eat about 70
aphids a day, but
the smaller male ladybug
only eats about 40 a day.

...there are more than 5,000 different
kinds of ladybugs. They are not all red
with black spots— some are black
with red spots...

...or yellow with black spots, or red
with yellow-and-black spots....

...these are 7-spot ladybugs,
but you might see a 2-spot or a
5-spot or even a yellow-and-black 22-spot.

...ladybugs are not
dangerous to humans—but they can bite.

...animals and birds won't eat ladybugs
because they taste
terrible.